HOW TO BE
A
GREAT BOSS
AND
TEAM LEADER

"Leading with Excellence: Mastering the Art of Effective Leadership"

VINCENT CLARK

Copyright ©

Dedication

To the countless leaders who tirelessly strive to empower, inspire, and uplift those they lead, this book is dedicated. Your unwavering commitment to excellence and dedication to nurturing the potential of your team members is an inspiration to us all. Through your guidance and mentorship, you shape not only individuals but entire organizations, fostering growth, innovation, and success. May this book serve as a tribute to your relentless pursuit of greatness and as a valuable resource to support you on your journey to becoming an even greater boss and team leader. Your impact is immeasurable, and your dedication is truly commendable.

Table of Contents

Acknowledgments

I extend my deepest gratitude to all those who have contributed to the creation of this book. Special thanks to my mentors and colleagues whose insights and support have enriched the content. I am immensely grateful to the team members who have shared their experiences, wisdom, and perspectives, enriching the book with diverse viewpoints. I also express appreciation to my family and friends for their unwavering encouragement and understanding throughout this journey. Additionally, I acknowledge the invaluable guidance and expertise of the editors, designers, and publishing professionals who have helped bring this project to fruition. This book is a collective effort, and I am thankful for every contribution.

Preface

Welcome to "How to Be a Great Boss and Team Leader." In today's dynamic and fast-paced work environments, effective leadership and team management skills are essential for success. This book is designed to provide practical guidance and insights to help you navigate the challenges of leadership and develop the qualities needed to become a great boss and team leader.

Throughout these pages, you'll discover strategies for building a positive workplace culture, mastering communication skills, motivating your team, resolving conflicts, and fostering personal growth as a leader. Whether you're a seasoned manager or aspiring to lead a team, this book offers valuable tools and techniques to enhance your leadership capabilities and achieve outstanding results.

I invite you to embark on this journey of self-discovery and growth as we explore what it truly means to be a great boss and team leader.

Chapter 1:

Understanding Leadership

- Defining Leadership

Leadership is a complex and multifaceted concept that defies a singular definition. At its core, leadership involves the ability to influence and inspire others towards a shared vision or goal. It encompasses a range of qualities and behaviors, including but not limited to vision, integrity, empathy, communication, and decisiveness. While traditional views of leadership often emphasize authority and control, modern perspectives highlight the importance of collaboration, empowerment, and servant leadership.

Effective leaders are adept at navigating challenges, fostering innovation, and maximizing the potential of their teams. They possess the humility to listen to diverse perspectives, the courage to make difficult decisions, and the resilience to adapt to changing circumstances. Moreover, leadership extends beyond formal roles and titles; it can emerge at any level of an organization or community.

Ultimately, leadership is not defined by one's position or authority but by the positive impact they have on others and the ability to inspire meaningful change. By embracing a growth mindset and continuously honing their skills, individuals can cultivate the qualities of effective leadership and make a lasting difference in their spheres of influence.

- Traits of Effective Leaders

Effective leaders possess a diverse array of traits that enable them to inspire, guide, and empower their teams. Among these traits are:

1. Vision: Effective leaders have a clear vision of the future and can articulate it compellingly, inspiring others to work towards common goals.

2. Integrity: Leaders with integrity uphold ethical principles and lead by example, earning the trust and respect of their team members.

3. Empathy: Understanding the perspectives and emotions of others allows effective leaders to connect on a deeper level, foster collaboration, and support individual growth.

4. Communication: Strong communication skills are essential for leaders to convey their

vision, provide feedback, and ensure alignment within the team.

5. Decisiveness: Making timely and well-informed decisions, even in the face of uncertainty, is a hallmark of effective leadership.

6. Adaptability: Effective leaders are flexible and adaptable, able to navigate change and overcome challenges with resilience and creativity.

7. Empowerment: Instead of micromanaging, effective leaders empower their team members by delegating tasks, providing resources, and fostering autonomy and accountability.

8. Emotional Intelligence: Leaders with high emotional intelligence can manage their own emotions and navigate interpersonal dynamics with empathy and self-awareness.

9. Resilience: Facing setbacks and adversity with resilience, effective leaders remain

steadfast in their commitment to their goals and inspire others to persevere.

10. Lifelong Learning: Effective leaders prioritize continuous learning and self-improvement, seeking feedback and staying abreast of industry trends and best practices.

By embodying these traits and continually developing their leadership skills, individuals can cultivate the qualities necessary to lead with impact and achieve success in their respective roles.

- Different Leadership Styles

Leadership styles vary depending on the individual leader's personality, the nature of the organization, and the specific context. Here are some common leadership styles:

1. Autocratic Leadership:
   - In this style, the leader makes decisions independently without seeking input from team members.
   - It is characterized by clear direction and strict control over decision-making processes.
   - While it can be effective in certain situations requiring quick and decisive action, it may lead to disengagement and resentment among team members.

2. Democratic Leadership:
   - Democratic leaders involve team members in the decision-making process, soliciting input and feedback before making decisions.
   - This style fosters collaboration, creativity, and buy-in from team members, leading to higher levels of engagement and satisfaction.
   - However, it can be time-consuming and may result in slower decision-making processes.

3. Transformational Leadership:
   - Transformational leaders inspire and motivate their teams by articulating a compelling vision and empowering them to achieve it.

- They lead by example, fostering a culture of trust, innovation, and continuous improvement.
- This style can drive significant organizational change and lead to high levels of employee engagement and performance.

4. Servant Leadership:
- Servant leaders prioritize the well-being and development of their team members, placing their needs above their own.
- They lead with humility, empathy, and a commitment to serving others, rather than seeking power or recognition.
- This style builds strong relationships, trust, and loyalty among team members, resulting in a highly cohesive and motivated workforce.

5. Laissez-Faire Leadership:
- Laissez-faire leaders adopt a hands-off approach, allowing team members to make decisions and manage their work independently.
- While it can promote autonomy and creativity, this style may lead to confusion, lack

of direction, and inconsistent outcomes without proper guidance and support from the leader.

Effective leaders are adaptable and may employ different leadership styles depending on the situation, leveraging the strengths of each approach to achieve the best outcomes for their teams and organizations.

Chapter 2:

Building a Positive Workplace Culture

- Importance of Workplace Culture

Workplace culture plays a crucial role in shaping the overall environment, morale, and performance of an organization. Here's why it's important:

1. Employee Engagement and Retention: A positive workplace culture fosters a sense of belonging, purpose, and fulfillment among employees, leading to higher levels of engagement and retention. When employees feel valued, supported, and appreciated, they are more likely to remain committed to the organization.

2. Productivity and Performance: A healthy workplace culture promotes collaboration, innovation, and high performance. When employees feel empowered to share ideas, take risks, and collaborate with colleagues, they are more likely to perform at their best and contribute to the organization's success.

3. Attraction of Top Talent: A positive workplace culture acts as a magnet for top talent, attracting skilled professionals who align with the organization's values and mission. When potential employees see that an organization prioritizes employee well-being, professional development, and a positive work environment, they are more likely to choose to join the team.

4. Employee Well-Being and Satisfaction: A supportive workplace culture promotes employee well-being by prioritizing work-life balance, mental health support, and a healthy work environment. When employees feel cared for and supported by their organization, they experience higher levels of job satisfaction and overall happiness.

5. Organizational Reputation and Brand Image: A strong workplace culture enhances the organization's reputation and brand image, both internally and externally. Positive word-of-mouth from satisfied employees can attract customers, partners, and stakeholders, while a negative culture can damage the organization's reputation and hinder growth.

6. Adaptability and Resilience: A positive workplace culture encourages adaptability, resilience, and continuous improvement. When employees feel safe to experiment, learn from failures, and embrace change, the organization becomes more agile and better equipped to navigate challenges and seize opportunities in a rapidly evolving business landscape.

However, workplace culture is a foundational element of organizational success, influencing employee engagement, productivity, talent acquisition, and overall performance. By prioritizing the development of a positive and inclusive culture, organizations can create environments where employees thrive, innovate, and contribute their best work.

- Creating a Positive Work Environment

Creating a positive work environment is essential for fostering employee satisfaction, productivity, and overall well-being. Here are key strategies to achieve this:

1. Clear Communication: Establish open and transparent communication channels to ensure that employees feel heard, informed, and valued. Encourage feedback, provide regular updates, and actively listen to employee concerns and suggestions.

2. Supportive Leadership: Cultivate a leadership style that is supportive, approachable, and empathetic. Leaders should prioritize employee development, recognize achievements, and provide guidance and mentorship when needed.

3. Recognition and Appreciation: Recognize and appreciate employees for their contributions and achievements. Celebrate

milestones, provide praise and rewards, and create a culture of appreciation that motivates and inspires team members.

4. Work-Life Balance: Promote work-life balance by offering flexible work arrangements, promoting time off, and discouraging overwork. Encourage employees to prioritize self-care, family time, and hobbies outside of work.

5. Opportunities for Growth: Provide opportunities for professional growth and development, including training programs, mentorship opportunities, and career advancement pathways. Invest in employees' skills and talents to help them reach their full potential.

6. Team Building Activities: Foster a sense of camaraderie and teamwork through team-building activities, social events, and collaborative projects. Encourage collaboration, mutual support, and a sense of belonging among team members.

7. Wellness Initiatives: Implement wellness initiatives and programs that support employees' physical, mental, and emotional well-being. Offer resources such as fitness classes, mindfulness workshops, and access to mental health support services.

8. Diversity and Inclusion: Promote diversity and inclusion in the workplace by embracing different perspectives, experiences, and backgrounds. Create a culture of respect, acceptance, and belonging where all employees feel valued and included.

9. Positive Feedback Culture: Encourage a culture of constructive feedback and continuous improvement. Provide regular feedback to employees on their performance, strengths, and areas for growth, and encourage them to do the same for their peers.

10. Lead by Example: As a leader, embody the values and behaviors you wish to see in your team members. Lead by example, demonstrate integrity, positivity, and resilience, and set the

tone for a positive and supportive work environment.

By implementing these strategies, organizations can create a positive work environment where employees feel motivated, engaged, and empowered to do their best work.

- Strategies for Fostering Team Collaboration

Effective team collaboration is essential for achieving organizational goals and driving innovation. Here are some strategies to foster collaboration among team members:

1. Clear Goals and Objectives: Ensure that team members have a shared understanding of the team's goals, objectives, and priorities. Clarify expectations, define roles and responsibilities, and establish clear benchmarks for success.

2. Open Communication Channels: Create open and transparent communication channels to facilitate collaboration and information sharing. Encourage regular team meetings, use collaboration tools such as messaging platforms and project management software, and provide opportunities for both formal and informal communication.

3. Foster a Culture of Trust: Build trust among team members by promoting transparency, honesty, and mutual respect. Encourage open dialogue, value diverse perspectives, and create a safe environment where team members feel comfortable expressing their ideas and opinions.

4. Encourage Collaboration Tools and Technologies: Provide access to collaboration tools and technologies that facilitate communication, file sharing, and project management. Utilize tools such as video conferencing, cloud storage, and collaborative editing platforms to streamline workflows and enhance productivity.

5. Establish Team Norms and Guidelines: Define team norms and guidelines that govern how team members interact and collaborate. Establish ground rules for communication, decision-making processes, and conflict resolution to ensure consistency and accountability.

6. Foster a Culture of Collaboration: Encourage a culture of collaboration by recognizing and rewarding collaborative behaviors. Celebrate team successes, acknowledge individual contributions, and promote a sense of shared ownership and accountability for outcomes.

7. Facilitate Team-Building Activities: Organize team-building activities and exercises to strengthen relationships, build trust, and enhance collaboration among team members. Activities such as team retreats, problem-solving workshops, and group outings can foster camaraderie and cohesion.

8. Promote Cross-Functional Collaboration: Encourage collaboration across departments, teams, and functional areas to leverage diverse

expertise and perspectives. Facilitate cross-functional meetings, projects, and initiatives to break down silos and promote knowledge sharing and innovation.

9. Provide Training and Development Opportunities: Offer training and development opportunities that enhance collaboration skills, such as communication, conflict resolution, and teamwork. Invest in team-building workshops, leadership development programs, and interpersonal skills training to empower team members to collaborate effectively.

10. Lead by Example: As a leader, model collaborative behavior and set the tone for teamwork and cooperation. Demonstrate active listening, seek input from team members, and encourage collaboration through your actions and behaviors.

By implementing these strategies, organizations can create a collaborative work environment where team members are empowered to work together towards common goals, drive innovation, and achieve success.

Chapter 3:

Effective Communication Skills

- Importance of Communication in Leadership

Communication is a cornerstone of effective leadership, serving as a linchpin for building trust, fostering collaboration, and driving organizational success. Here's why communication is paramount in leadership:

1. Vision Clarity: Leaders must effectively communicate their vision, goals, and expectations to inspire and align team members toward a common purpose. Clear and compelling communication helps employees

understand the organization's direction and their role in achieving its objectives.

2. Alignment and Consistency: Communication ensures alignment across all levels of the organization, promoting consistency in messaging and decision-making. When leaders communicate transparently and consistently, they foster trust and confidence among employees, leading to greater engagement and commitment.

3. Relationship Building: Effective communication strengthens relationships between leaders and their teams by fostering open dialogue, active listening, and mutual respect. Leaders who communicate authentically and empathetically build rapport with their team members, creating a supportive and inclusive work environment.

4. Conflict Resolution: Communication skills are crucial for resolving conflicts and addressing issues that arise within teams. Leaders who can navigate difficult conversations, provide constructive feedback,

and facilitate dialogue among conflicting parties can mitigate tensions and promote a culture of collaboration and cooperation.

5. Empowerment and Engagement: Clear communication empowers employees by keeping them informed, involved, and engaged in decision-making processes. When employees feel valued and heard, they are more likely to contribute their ideas, take ownership of their work, and remain committed to the organization's goals.

6. Change Management: Effective communication is essential during periods of change and uncertainty, such as organizational restructuring, mergers, or shifts in strategy. Leaders who communicate openly, honestly, and empathetically can help alleviate fears, address concerns and rally employees around a shared vision for the future.

7. Innovation and Creativity: Communication fosters an environment where diverse perspectives are valued and ideas can flourish. Leaders who encourage open dialogue,

brainstorming sessions, and knowledge sharing inspire innovation and creativity within their teams, driving continuous improvement and competitive advantage.

8. Performance Management: Communication plays a vital role in providing feedback, setting expectations, and recognizing achievements. Leaders who communicate performance expectations clearly and provide timely feedback empower employees to excel and grow professionally.

In summary, effective communication is indispensable for leadership success, enabling leaders to inspire, engage, and empower their teams to achieve extraordinary results. By honing their communication skills and prioritizing transparent and authentic communication, leaders can cultivate a culture of trust, collaboration, and excellence within their organizations.

- Active Listening Techniques

Active listening is a critical communication skill that enables leaders to understand, empathize with, and connect with their team members. Here are some techniques to enhance active listening:

1. Maintain Eye Contact: Maintain eye contact with the speaker to demonstrate attentiveness and show that you are fully engaged in the conversation.

2. Provide Nonverbal Cues: Use nonverbal cues such as nodding, smiling, and leaning forward to signal that you are actively listening and encouraging the speaker to continue.

3. Avoid Interrupting: Resist the urge to interrupt or interject while the speaker is talking. Instead, allow them to express themselves fully before responding.

4. Paraphrase and Summarize: Paraphrase what the speaker has said in your own words to ensure understanding and clarify any points of confusion. Summarize key points to demonstrate that you have been actively listening.

5. Ask Open-Ended Questions: Encourage further elaboration and exploration by asking open-ended questions that invite the speaker to share more about their thoughts, feelings, and experiences.

6. Reflect Feelings: Reflect on the speaker's emotions and feelings by acknowledging and validating their experiences. For example, you might say, "It sounds like you're feeling frustrated about the situation."

7. Practice Empathy: Put yourself in the speaker's shoes and try to understand their perspective and emotions. Show empathy by expressing understanding and compassion for their experiences.

8. Minimize Distractions: Eliminate distractions and focus your full attention on the speaker. Turn off electronic devices, close doors, and create a quiet and conducive environment for listening.

9. Be Patient and Present: Practice patience and be fully present in the moment, giving the speaker your undivided attention. Avoid multitasking or mentally preparing your response while the speaker is talking.

10. Validate and Affirm: Validate the speaker's thoughts and feelings by acknowledging their perspective and affirming their contributions to the conversation. Make them feel heard and valued.

By incorporating these active listening techniques into your communication style, you can build stronger relationships, foster trust, and enhance collaboration with your team members. Active listening is a powerful tool for effective leadership, enabling you to connect authentically with others and create a supportive and inclusive work environment.

- Giving and Receiving Constructive Feedback

Effective feedback is essential for personal and professional growth, fostering continuous improvement and development within teams. Here are some strategies for giving and receiving constructive feedback:

Giving Constructive Feedback:

1. Be Specific and Objective: Provide specific examples of behaviors or actions that you observed, focusing on objective facts rather than subjective opinions.

2. Focus on Behavior, Not Personality: Address the behavior or performance in question rather than making personal attacks or judgments about the individual.

3. Use the "Sandwich" Approach: Start with positive feedback or acknowledgment of strengths, followed by constructive criticism, and end with more positive reinforcement or encouragement.

4. Be Timely: Deliver feedback promptly, ideally soon after the observed behavior or

performance, to ensure relevance and effectiveness.

5. Be Empathetic: Consider the recipient's feelings and perspective when delivering feedback, and communicate in a respectful and empathetic manner.

6. Offer Solutions or Suggestions: Provide actionable recommendations or suggestions for improvement to help the recipient address the areas identified for development.

7. Encourage Dialogue: Invite the recipient to share their perspective, ask clarifying questions, and engage in a constructive dialogue to ensure mutual understanding.

8. Follow-up: Follow up on feedback discussions to monitor progress, offer support, and provide additional guidance or feedback as needed.

Receiving Constructive Feedback:

1. Be Open-Minded: Approach feedback with an open mind and a willingness to learn and grow. Avoid becoming defensive or dismissive of feedback, even if it is difficult to hear.

2. Listen Actively: Listen attentively to the feedback, seeking to understand the

perspectives and insights being shared. Avoid interrupting or jumping to conclusions.

3. Ask Clarifying Questions: Seek clarification if you are unsure about any aspect of the feedback, and ask for specific examples or suggestions for improvement.

4. Focus on Learning and Improvement: View feedback as an opportunity for learning and development rather than as criticism or judgment. Embrace feedback as a valuable tool for self-improvement.

5. Express Gratitude: Thank the giver for their feedback, acknowledging their efforts to help you grow and develop professionally.

6. Reflect and Take Action: Reflect on the feedback received, identify areas for improvement, and develop a plan of action to address them. Set specific goals and timelines for making progress.

7. Seek Support: Seek support from mentors, peers, or supervisors to help you implement changes and navigate challenges identified through feedback.

8. Follow Up: Follow up with the feedback giver to update them on your progress and

demonstrate your commitment to continuous improvement.

By embracing a culture of constructive feedback and practicing these strategies, leaders and team members can create an environment that promotes growth, learning, and excellence. Constructive feedback is a powerful tool for personal and professional development, enabling individuals and teams to reach their full potential and achieve success.

Chapter 4:

Motivating and Inspiring Your Team

- Understanding Motivation Theories

Motivation theories provide valuable insights into what drives human behavior and how leaders can effectively motivate and inspire their teams. Here are some key motivation theories to consider:

1. Maslow's Hierarchy of Needs: Maslow's theory suggests that individuals have a hierarchy of needs, starting with basic physiological needs such as food and shelter, followed by safety, belongingness, esteem, and self-actualization. Leaders can motivate employees by addressing their needs at each level of the hierarchy, creating a supportive work environment where employees feel

valued, respected, and empowered to achieve their full potential.

2. Herzberg's Two-Factor Theory: Herzberg proposed that there are two sets of factors that influence employee motivation and satisfaction: hygiene factors and motivators. Hygiene factors, such as salary, job security, and working conditions, are essential for preventing dissatisfaction but do not necessarily lead to motivation. Motivators, such as recognition, achievement, and growth opportunities, are intrinsic factors that drive motivation and job satisfaction. Leaders can motivate employees by focusing on providing meaningful work, recognition, and opportunities for personal and professional development.

3. Expectancy Theory: Expectancy theory posits that individuals are motivated to exert effort when they believe that their efforts will lead to desired outcomes and that they are capable of achieving those outcomes. According to this theory, motivation is influenced by three factors: expectancy (the belief that effort will lead to performance), instrumentality (the

belief that performance will lead to outcomes), and valence (value placed on the outcomes). Leaders can motivate employees by setting clear expectations, providing support and resources to help employees succeed, and aligning rewards with desired outcomes.

4. Equity Theory: Equity theory suggests that individuals compare their inputs (e.g., effort, time, skills) and outcomes (e.g., rewards, recognition) to those of others to assess fairness. When individuals perceive inequity, such as receiving less rewards for their efforts compared to others, they may feel demotivated and seek to restore equity. Leaders can motivate employees by ensuring fairness and transparency in reward systems, providing opportunities for input and participation, and addressing any perceived inequities in the workplace.

5. Goal-Setting Theory: Goal-setting theory proposes that setting specific, challenging goals can motivate individuals to perform at a higher level. According to this theory, goals should be specific, measurable, achievable, relevant, and

time-bound (SMART). Leaders can motivate employees by setting clear, meaningful goals, providing feedback and support to help employees achieve their goals, and celebrating successes along the way.

By understanding these motivation theories and applying their principles in the workplace, leaders can effectively motivate and inspire their teams to achieve exceptional results, foster engagement, and create a positive work environment conducive to success.

- Recognizing and Rewarding Achievements

Recognizing and rewarding achievements is essential for fostering a positive work environment, motivating employees, and reinforcing desired behaviors. Here are some strategies for effectively recognizing and rewarding achievements within your team:

1. Regular Feedback: Provide timely and specific feedback to acknowledge individual and team achievements. Recognize employees for their contributions, accomplishments, and efforts toward achieving organizational goals.

2. Public Recognition: Publicly recognize employees' achievements in team meetings, company-wide emails, or internal newsletters. Highlight their accomplishments and express appreciation for their hard work and dedication.

3. Personalized Recognition: Tailor recognition efforts to individual preferences and preferences. Some employees may prefer public recognition, while others may appreciate private acknowledgment or personalized tokens of appreciation.

4. Peer Recognition: Encourage peer-to-peer recognition by providing opportunities for team members to acknowledge and appreciate each other's contributions. Implement peer recognition programs or platforms where

employees can give and receive recognition from their colleagues.

5. Tangible Rewards: Offer tangible rewards such as bonuses, gift cards, or merchandise to celebrate significant achievements or milestones. Consider the preferences and interests of individual employees when selecting rewards to ensure they are meaningful and motivating.

6. Development Opportunities: Provide opportunities for professional development, such as training programs, conferences, or mentorship opportunities, to reward high performers and support their continued growth and advancement within the organization.

7. Flexibility and Benefits: Offer flexible work arrangements, additional time off, or other benefits as a reward for exceptional performance. Recognize employees' work-life balance needs and provide support to help them achieve their personal and professional goals.

8. Celebration Events: Organize celebration events or team outings to commemorate significant achievements, milestones, or project completions. Create opportunities for team members to come together, bond, and celebrate their successes.

9. Performance-Based Incentives: Implement performance-based incentive programs tied to specific goals, metrics, or key performance indicators. Reward employees who exceed expectations or achieve outstanding results with financial incentives or other rewards.

10. Continuous Recognition: Make recognition and appreciation a regular part of your team culture by incorporating it into daily routines and practices. Celebrate small wins, milestones, and progress towards goals to maintain momentum and motivation.

By implementing these strategies, leaders can create a culture of recognition and appreciation that motivates employees, fosters engagement, and drives performance. Recognizing and rewarding achievements not only boosts morale and satisfaction but also strengthens team cohesion and contributes to overall organizational success.

- Inspiring Team Members Toward a Common Goal

Inspiring team members toward a common goal is essential for achieving collective success and maximizing team performance. Here are some strategies to effectively inspire and align your team members toward a shared vision:

1. Communicate a Compelling Vision: Articulate a clear and compelling vision that outlines the purpose, values, and desired outcomes of the team. Communicate why the goal is important and how it aligns with the organization's mission and objectives.

2. Lead by Example: Demonstrate commitment, passion, and dedication to the team's goals and values through your actions and behaviors.

Lead by example, embodying the qualities and behaviors you wish to see in your team members.

3. Foster a Sense of Purpose: Help team members understand the significance of their work and how it contributes to the achievement of the team's goals and the organization's mission. Create a sense of purpose and meaning by connecting individual tasks to the broader objectives of the team.

4. Empower and Delegate: Empower team members by providing autonomy, ownership, and responsibility for their work. Delegate tasks and decision-making authority to enable team members to contribute their unique skills and expertise toward achieving the common goal.

5. Provide Support and Resources: Ensure that team members have the necessary support, resources, and tools to succeed in their roles. Remove obstacles and barriers that may hinder progress and provide guidance and assistance when needed.

6. Foster Collaboration and Teamwork: Encourage collaboration, communication, and mutual support among team members. Foster a culture of trust, respect, and inclusivity where team members feel valued and supported in working towards the common goal.

7. Celebrate Milestones and Successes: Recognize and celebrate achievements, milestones, and progress towards the common goal. Acknowledge the contributions of individual team members and the collective efforts of the team to maintain morale and motivation.

8. Provide Feedback and Coaching: Offer constructive feedback, guidance, and coaching to help team members grow and develop in their roles. Provide regular updates on performance, clarify expectations, and offer support to address any challenges or areas for improvement.

9. Encourage Innovation and Creativity: Foster a culture of innovation and creativity by encouraging team members to think outside the

box, take risks, and explore new ideas and solutions. Create an environment where experimentation and learning are valued and supported.

10. Stay Committed and Flexible: Stay committed to the common goal, even in the face of obstacles or setbacks. Remain flexible and adaptable, willing to adjust plans and strategies as needed to overcome challenges and keep the team on track toward achieving the desired outcomes.

By implementing these strategies, leaders can inspire and motivate team members to work collaboratively toward a common goal, driving engagement, performance, and success. A shared vision and a sense of purpose can unite team members, empower them to overcome obstacles and achieve extraordinary results together.

Chapter 5:

Conflict Resolution and Problem Solving

- Identifying Sources of Conflict

Conflict can arise in any team or organization due to various factors. Identifying the sources of conflict is crucial for effectively resolving issues and fostering a positive work environment. Here are some common sources of conflict in the workplace:

1. Differences in Goals and Priorities: Conflicts may arise when team members have different goals, priorities, or agendas. Misalignment in objectives can lead to competing interests and disagreements about how resources should be allocated or tasks should be prioritized.

2. Communication Breakdowns: Poor communication or misunderstandings can contribute to conflicts within teams. Lack of clarity, misinterpretation of messages, or ineffective communication channels can lead to confusion, frustration, and conflict among team members.

3. Personality Clashes: Differences in personalities, communication styles, and work preferences can lead to interpersonal conflicts within teams. Conflicting personalities or behaviors may create tension, resentment, or friction among team members.

4. Role Ambiguity: Unclear roles, responsibilities, or expectations can lead to conflicts within teams. When team members are unsure of their roles or feel that their contributions are undervalued, they may experience frustration or resentment towards others.

5. Resource Allocation: Limited resources, such as time, budget, or manpower, can be a source

of conflict within teams. Competition for resources or disagreements about how resources should be allocated can lead to tensions and conflicts among team members.

6. Organizational Changes: Changes in organizational structure, processes, or leadership can disrupt team dynamics and lead to conflicts. Uncertainty, resistance to change, or perceived injustices related to organizational changes can fuel conflicts within teams.

7. Workload Imbalance: Inequities in workload distribution or perceived favoritism can lead to conflicts within teams. When some team members feel overburdened or undervalued compared to others, it can create resentment and dissatisfaction.

8. Cultural Differences: Cultural diversity within teams can enrich collaboration but may also lead to conflicts due to differences in values, beliefs, or communication norms. Cultural misunderstandings or stereotypes can contribute to tension and conflict among team members.

9. Performance Issues: Differences in performance standards, work ethic, or quality of work can lead to conflicts within teams. When some team members fail to meet expectations or contribute to shared goals, it can create frustration and resentment among others.

10. External Pressures: External factors such as tight deadlines, demanding clients or market competition can increase stress and tension within teams, leading to conflicts. Pressure to deliver results under challenging circumstances may exacerbate conflicts and strain relationships among team members.

By recognizing and addressing the sources of conflict within teams, leaders can proactively manage conflicts, promote constructive dialogue, and foster a collaborative and harmonious work environment. Effective conflict resolution strategies and open communication can help mitigate conflicts and promote teamwork, innovation, and organizational success.

- Strategies for Managing Conflict

Conflict is a natural and inevitable part of any workplace, but effective conflict management can turn disagreements into opportunities for growth and collaboration. Here are some strategies for managing conflict in the workplace:

1. Address Issues Early: Encourage open communication and address conflicts promptly before they escalate. Deal with issues as soon as they arise to prevent them from festering and becoming more challenging to resolve.

2. Listen Actively: Practice active listening to understand the perspectives and concerns of all parties involved in the conflict. Allow each person to express their thoughts and feelings without interruption, and demonstrate empathy and respect for their viewpoints.

3. Foster Respectful Communication: Establish ground rules for communication that promote

respect, civility, and constructive dialogue. Encourage team members to communicate assertively, express their needs and concerns respectfully, and refrain from personal attacks or blame.

4. Find Common Ground: Identify shared interests or goals that both parties can agree upon and use as a foundation for finding solutions. Focus on areas of agreement and mutual benefit to build rapport and facilitate compromise.

5. Collaborative Problem-Solving: Encourage collaborative problem-solving by involving all parties in the process of finding solutions. Brainstorm potential solutions together, weigh the pros and cons of each option, and work towards finding a mutually acceptable resolution.

6. Use Mediation or Facilitation: Consider involving a neutral third party, such as a mediator or facilitator, to help facilitate communication, clarify misunderstandings, and guide the conflict resolution process. An

impartial mediator can help parties explore their interests and find common ground.

7. Practice Empathy and Perspective-Taking: Encourage empathy and perspective-taking by asking team members to put themselves in each other's shoes. Help individuals understand the underlying motivations, concerns, and emotions driving the conflict to foster empathy and understanding.

8. Focus on Solutions, Not Blame: Shift the focus away from assigning blame and towards finding constructive solutions to the underlying issues. Encourage a problem-solving mindset that focuses on addressing root causes and moving forward collaboratively.

9. Set Clear Expectations: Clarify expectations around roles, responsibilities, and communication to prevent misunderstandings and conflicts from arising in the future. Establish clear guidelines for decision-making processes, conflict resolution procedures, and acceptable behavior in the workplace.

10. Follow Up and Monitor Progress: Follow up with all parties involved in the conflict to ensure that agreed-upon solutions are implemented effectively and to monitor progress over time. Provide support and guidance as needed to address any lingering issues or concerns.

By implementing these strategies for managing conflict effectively, leaders can promote a positive work environment, strengthen relationships, and foster collaboration and teamwork within their teams. Conflict can be an opportunity for growth and learning when approached constructively and managed with empathy and respect.

- Problem-Solving Techniques for Team Leaders

As a team leader, mastering problem-solving techniques is essential for overcoming challenges, fostering innovation, and driving organizational success. Here are some effective problem-solving techniques for team leaders:

1. Define the Problem: Clearly define the problem or challenge that needs to be addressed. Encourage team members to gather relevant information, identify root causes, and understand the scope and impact of the problem.

2. Brainstorming: Facilitate brainstorming sessions to generate a wide range of ideas and potential solutions to the problem. Encourage creativity, suspend judgment, and explore both conventional and unconventional approaches to problem-solving.

3. Analytical Thinking: Use analytical thinking techniques, such as root cause analysis, SWOT analysis (Strengths, Weaknesses, Opportunities, Threats), or Fishbone diagrams, to identify underlying causes, contributing factors, and potential solutions to the problem.

4. Decision-Making Frameworks: Utilize decision-making frameworks, such as cost-benefit analysis, risk assessment, or decision trees, to evaluate potential solutions and make informed decisions. Consider the potential benefits, risks, and trade-offs associated with each option.

5. Collaborative Problem-Solving: Foster collaboration and teamwork by involving team members in the problem-solving process. Encourage diverse perspectives, leverage the collective expertise of the team, and promote open dialogue and knowledge sharing.

6. Pilot Testing: Implement pilot tests or small-scale experiments to test potential solutions in a controlled environment before full implementation. Gather feedback, evaluate

outcomes, and refine solutions based on lessons learned from the pilot phase.

7. Break the Problem Down: Break the problem down into smaller, more manageable components and prioritize areas for action. Addressing smaller aspects of the problem incrementally can make the problem-solving process more manageable and increase the likelihood of success.

8. Stakeholder Engagement: Engage key stakeholders, such as clients, customers, or other relevant parties, in the problem-solving process. Solicit their input, gather feedback on proposed solutions, and ensure alignment with their needs and expectations.

9. Continuous Improvement: Embrace a mindset of continuous improvement by seeking feedback, evaluating outcomes, and learning from both successes and failures. Encourage a culture of experimentation, adaptation, and resilience in the face of challenges.

10. Celebrate Successes: Recognize and celebrate successes along the way to motivate and inspire team members. Acknowledge the contributions of individuals and teams to the problem-solving process, and reinforce a culture of collaboration and innovation.

By applying these problem-solving techniques, team leaders can effectively navigate challenges, drive innovation, and empower their teams to achieve exceptional results. Problem-solving is a critical skill for leadership success, enabling leaders to overcome obstacles, seize opportunities, and lead their teams toward a brighter future.

Chapter 6:

Personal Growth and Continuous Improvement

- Self-Reflection for Leadership Development

Self-reflection is a powerful tool for leadership development, enabling leaders to gain insight into their strengths, weaknesses, and areas for growth. Here are some self-reflection exercises that leaders can use to enhance their personal growth and continuous improvement:

1. Clarify Your Values and Principles: Reflect on your core values, beliefs, and principles that guide your leadership style and decision-making. Consider how well-aligned your actions are with your values and identify any areas where you may need to make adjustments.

2. Assess Your Strengths and Weaknesses: Take stock of your strengths, talents, and areas of expertise as a leader. Identify areas where you excel and leverage these strengths to maximize your impact. Similarly, acknowledge your weaknesses or areas for improvement and develop strategies to address them.

3. Reflect on Past Experiences: Think back on past leadership experiences, both successes and failures and consider what you have learned from them. Reflect on the challenges you faced, how you responded to them, and what you could have done differently. Extract valuable lessons from these experiences to inform your future leadership approach.

4. Seek Feedback from Others: Solicit feedback from colleagues, mentors, or team members to gain different perspectives on your leadership style and performance. Listen attentively to constructive criticism and use it as an opportunity for self-reflection and growth.

5. Set Clear Goals for Development: Define specific goals and objectives for your leadership

development based on your self-reflection and feedback. Identify areas where you want to improve or develop new skills and create a plan of action to achieve these goals.

6. Practice Mindfulness and Self-Awareness: Cultivate mindfulness and self-awareness through practices such as meditation, journaling, or regular self-check-ins. Pay attention to your thoughts, emotions, and reactions in various leadership situations, and use this awareness to make intentional choices and responses.

7. Embrace a Growth Mindset: Adopt a growth mindset that embraces challenges, sees setbacks as opportunities for learning, and values ongoing development. Embrace the belief that your abilities and skills can be developed through dedication, effort, and perseverance.

8. Experiment with Different Leadership Approaches: Be open to experimenting with different leadership approaches and styles to see what works best for you and your team.

Explore new strategies, techniques, and behaviors, and be willing to adapt and evolve based on feedback and results.

9. Practice Empathy and Active Listening: Reflect on your ability to empathize with others and actively listen to their perspectives and concerns. Consider how well you understand and respond to the needs and emotions of your team members, and seek to deepen your connections through empathy and active listening.

10. Reflect Regularly and Adjust as Needed: Make self-reflection a regular practice in your leadership journey, setting aside time on a daily, weekly, or monthly basis to reflect on your experiences, progress, and challenges. Adjust your approach as needed based on your reflections and insights, continuously striving for personal growth and improvement.

By engaging in regular self-reflection, leaders can deepen their self-awareness, enhance their leadership effectiveness, and continue to evolve and grow in their roles. Personal growth and continuous improvement are ongoing processes that require self-awareness, commitment, and a willingness to learn and adapt.

- Setting and Achieving Personal and Professional Goals

Setting and achieving personal and professional goals is essential for growth, fulfillment, and success in both aspects of life. Here are some strategies to effectively set and achieve your goals:

1. Define Your Goals: Start by clearly defining your personal and professional goals. Ensure that your goals are specific, measurable, achievable, relevant, and time-bound (SMART). Identify what you want to accomplish and why it's important to you.

2. Prioritize Your Goals: Evaluate your goals and prioritize them based on their importance, urgency, and potential impact. Focus on the goals that align with your values, aspirations, and long-term vision for personal and professional fulfillment.

3. Break Down Your Goals: Break down larger, long-term goals into smaller, actionable steps or milestones. Breaking goals into manageable tasks makes them more attainable and helps you track progress along the way.

4. Create a Plan of Action: Develop a detailed plan of action outlining the specific steps you need to take to achieve each goal. Set deadlines, allocate resources, and identify potential obstacles or challenges that may arise.

5. Stay Organized and Disciplined: Stay organized and disciplined in pursuing your goals by establishing routines, schedules, and systems to keep yourself on track. Use tools such as calendars, to-do lists, or productivity apps to manage your time effectively and prioritize tasks.

6. Monitor Progress and Adjust as Needed: Regularly monitor your progress towards your goals and adjust your approach as needed. Celebrate milestones and successes along the way, but also be willing to reassess and modify your plans if you encounter setbacks or obstacles.

7. Stay Motivated and Inspired: Stay motivated and inspired by regularly revisiting your goals, reminding yourself of your reasons for pursuing them, and visualizing your success. Surround yourself with supportive peers, mentors, or role models who can encourage and inspire you along your journey.

8. Seek Feedback and Support: Seek feedback from others, such as mentors, peers, or trusted advisors, to gain different perspectives and insights on your goals and progress. Leverage their expertise and support to overcome challenges and stay accountable.

9. Practice Self-Care and Well-Being: Prioritize self-care and well-being as you pursue your

goals by maintaining a healthy work-life balance, managing stress effectively, and prioritizing activities that recharge and energize you.

10. Reflect and Celebrate Achievements: Take time to reflect on your achievements and celebrate your successes, both big and small. Acknowledge the progress you've made, the lessons you've learned, and the growth you've experienced along the way.

By following these strategies and staying committed to your goals, you can effectively set and achieve your personal and professional aspirations, leading to a more fulfilling and successful life. Remember that goal setting is a continuous process, and it's okay to adjust your goals as your priorities and circumstances evolve.

- Building Resilience and Adaptability as a Leader

Resilience and adaptability are essential qualities for leaders to navigate challenges, setbacks, and change effectively. Here are some strategies to build resilience and adaptability as a leader:

1. Cultivate a Growth Mindset: Embrace a growth mindset that views challenges as opportunities for learning and growth. Adopt the belief that you can develop your skills, overcome obstacles, and adapt to new situations through effort and perseverance.

2. Develop Self-Awareness: Foster self-awareness by regularly reflecting on your thoughts, emotions, and reactions to different situations. Understand your strengths, weaknesses, and triggers, and use this awareness to manage stress, regulate emotions, and make informed decisions.

3. Practice Flexibility and Agility: Be flexible and adaptable in your approach to leadership and problem-solving. Embrace change as a natural part of the leadership journey and be willing to adjust your plans, strategies, and priorities as needed in response to evolving circumstances.

4. Build Resilience through Adversity: Embrace challenges and setbacks as opportunities to build resilience and strength. View failures as learning experiences, extract valuable lessons from adversity, and use setbacks as fuel for growth and improvement.

5. Foster a Supportive Network: Surround yourself with a supportive network of colleagues, mentors, friends, and family who can provide encouragement, guidance, and perspective during challenging times. Lean on your support system for advice, feedback, and emotional support when needed.

6. Practice Self-Care: Prioritize self-care and well-being to sustain your energy and resilience as a leader. Make time for activities that

recharge and rejuvenate you, such as exercise, hobbies, relaxation techniques, or spending time with loved ones.

7. Develop Coping Strategies: Develop healthy coping strategies to manage stress, adversity, and uncertainty effectively. Practice mindfulness, deep breathing exercises, or other stress management techniques to stay grounded and centered during challenging times.

8. Foster a Positive Work Culture: Create a positive work culture that promotes resilience, adaptability, and mutual support among team members. Encourage open communication, collaboration, and empathy, and celebrate resilience and perseverance in the face of adversity.

9. Set Realistic Expectations: Set realistic expectations for yourself and others, recognizing that perfection is not attainable and mistakes are growth opportunities. Be kind to yourself and others, and foster a culture of

experimentation, learning, and continuous improvement.

10. Lead by Example: Lead by example and demonstrate resilience and adaptability in your behavior and actions. Show vulnerability, acknowledge challenges openly, and model healthy coping strategies and problem-solving techniques for your team to follow.

By practicing these strategies, leaders can cultivate resilience and adaptability, enabling them to thrive in the face of adversity, lead with confidence, and inspire others to do the same. Resilient and adaptable leaders are better equipped to navigate uncertainty, overcome obstacles, and lead their teams to success in an ever-changing world.

Conclusion:

In the dynamic landscape of leadership, one constant remains: the necessity for resilience and adaptability. Throughout this exploration, we've delved into the essential qualities and strategies that empower leaders to navigate challenges, inspire their teams, and drive success in the face of uncertainty and change.

Resilience, the ability to bounce back from setbacks, and adaptability, the capacity to adjust to new circumstances, are indispensable attributes for leaders in today's fast-paced world. As leaders encounter obstacles, setbacks, and unforeseen circumstances, their ability to maintain composure, persevere through adversity, and pivot in response to change becomes paramount.

Building resilience and adaptability as a leader is not a one-time endeavor but rather an ongoing journey of growth and development. It requires self-awareness, a growth mindset, and a willingness to embrace challenges as opportunities for learning and growth. Leaders must cultivate resilience through adversity, leveraging setbacks as opportunities to strengthen their resolve, deepen their self-awareness, and refine their leadership approach.

Adaptability, likewise, is a skill that leaders must continuously cultivate, honing their ability to navigate uncertainty, complexity, and ambiguity with confidence and agility. In an ever-changing business environment, leaders must be prepared to pivot, innovate, and reinvent themselves and their organizations to stay ahead of the curve.

Throughout this journey, leaders can draw upon a toolkit of strategies and practices to build resilience and adaptability:

- Cultivating self-awareness through reflection, feedback, and mindfulness practices.
- Embracing a growth mindset that sees challenges as opportunities for growth and improvement.
- Seeking support from a network of mentors, peers, and trusted advisors.
- Prioritizing self-care and well-being to sustain energy and resilience.
- Fostering a positive work culture that promotes collaboration, innovation, and mutual support.

- Leading by example, demonstrating resilience and adaptability in their behavior and actions.

As leaders embody these qualities and practices, they not only enhance their effectiveness but also inspire and empower those around them. Resilient and adaptable leaders serve as beacons of strength and stability, guiding their teams through turbulent times with confidence, optimism, and resilience.

In conclusion, resilience and adaptability are not just skills to be cultivated; they are mindsets to be embraced and embodied. By fostering resilience and adaptability within themselves and their teams, leaders can navigate challenges, seize opportunities, and lead their organizations to success in an ever-changing world.

As we embark on the journey of leadership, let us remember that resilience and adaptability are not just tools in our arsenal but virtues to be cultivated, strengths to be honed, and legacies to be embraced. With resilience as our anchor and adaptability as our compass, we can chart a course toward a brighter future, inspiring others to follow in our footsteps and leaving a lasting impact on the world around us.

Conclusion

In the dynamic landscape of leadership, one constant remains: the necessity for resilience and adaptability. Throughout this exploration, we've delved into the essential qualities and strategies that empower leaders to navigate challenges, inspire their teams, and drive success in the face of uncertainty and change.

Resilience, the ability to bounce back from setbacks, and adaptability, the capacity to adjust to new circumstances, are indispensable attributes for leaders in today's fast-paced world. As leaders encounter obstacles, setbacks, and unforeseen circumstances, their ability to maintain composure, persevere through adversity, and pivot in response to change becomes paramount.

Building resilience and adaptability as a leader is not a one-time endeavor but rather an ongoing journey of growth and development. It requires self-awareness, a growth mindset, and a willingness to embrace challenges as opportunities for learning and growth. Leaders must cultivate resilience through adversity, leveraging setbacks as opportunities to strengthen their resolve, deepen their self-awareness, and refine their leadership approach.

Adaptability, likewise, is a skill that leaders must continuously cultivate, honing their ability to navigate uncertainty, complexity, and ambiguity with confidence and agility. In an ever-changing business environment, leaders must be prepared to pivot, innovate, and reinvent themselves and their organizations to stay ahead of the curve.

Throughout this journey, leaders can draw upon a toolkit of strategies and practices to build resilience and adaptability:

- Cultivating self-awareness through reflection, feedback, and mindfulness practices.
- Embracing a growth mindset that sees challenges as opportunities for growth and improvement.

- Seeking support from a network of mentors, peers, and trusted advisors.
- Prioritizing self-care and well-being to sustain energy and resilience.
- Fostering a positive work culture that promotes collaboration, innovation, and mutual support.
- Leading by example, demonstrating resilience and adaptability in their own behavior and actions.

As leaders embody these qualities and practices, they not only enhance their own effectiveness but also inspire and empower those around them. Resilient and adaptable leaders serve as beacons of strength and stability, guiding their teams through turbulent times with confidence, optimism, and resilience.

In conclusion, resilience and adaptability are not just skills to be cultivated; they are mindsets to be embraced and embodied. By fostering resilience and adaptability within themselves and their teams, leaders can navigate challenges, seize opportunities, and lead their organizations to success in an ever-changing world.

As we embark on the journey of leadership, let us remember that resilience and adaptability are not just tools in our arsenal but virtues to be cultivated, strengths to be honed, and legacies to be embraced. With resilience as our anchor and adaptability as our compass, we can chart a course towards a brighter future, inspiring others to follow in our footsteps and leaving a lasting impact on the world around us.

How To Be a Great Boss And Team Leader

How To Be a Great Boss And Team Leader